EVEN MORE
WESSEX WALKIES
for you and your dog

Dedicated to my dog Bounty - and not forgetting
Belle, Benji, Rover, Jessica and all the other doggie
friends we have made through these books

The eager little face, the hopeful tail
Shall it be forest, field or hidden lane
Who could resist them? Let's abandon work
And so, at last, it's 'Walkies!' time again.

Patricia M Wilnecker
1996

By the same author

non-fiction
High Street Murders 1598
Published by Poole Museum Services

A History of Upper Parkstone (beginning to 1939)
Upper Parkstone in the Second World War
More Recollections of Old Upper Parkstone
Bounty, the tale of a dog
Wessex Walkies for you and your dog
More Wessex Walkies for you and your dog
Ghostly Tales of Wessex
Published by Patricia M Wilnecker

fiction:
The Bountifull Gyfte
Published by Patricia M Wilnecker

Published by Patricia M Wilnecker
73 Gwynne Road
Parkstone
Poole
Dorset
BH12 2AR

First published 1996
© P M Wilnecker

British Library Cataloguing in Publication Data
A catalogue record for this book is available from the British Library

All rights reserved
ISBN 0 9513971 8 4

Made and printed in Great Britain by The Local History Press, 3 Devonshire Promenade, Lenton, Nottingham NG7 2DS

CONTENTS

		PAGE
Introduction		5

A map showing the locations of the walks can be found on pages 18 and 19

WALK	LOCATION	PAGE
1	Lepe Country Park	6
2	Beaulieu to Bucklers Hard	6
3	Ivy Wood, nr Brockenhurst	7
4	Boltons Bench, Lyndhurst	7
5	Janesmoor Pond, Stoney Cross	8
6	Stockbridge Down	8
7	Millyford Bridge, nr Lyndhurst	8
8	Oakley, New Forest	9
9	Burley, opposite golf club	9
10	Brownhills, Holmesley	9
11	Long Meadow/Barton Common, Barton-on-Sea	10
12	Danes Stream, Milford-on-Sea	10
13	Ringwood Forest, by Blue Haze Pets Hotel	10
14	Avon Valley Tramway	11
15	Fishermans Bank, Stanpit	11
16	Druitt Gardens, Christchurch	12
17	Woodland Walk, Boscombe	12
18	Muscliffe Arboretum	12
19	Parkstone 'Lakes'	13
20	Constitution Hill Viewpoint, Parkstone	13
21	Baiter to Poole Quay	13
22	Parrs Plantation, Poole	13
23	Knighton Heath, by golf course	14
24	Happy Bottom, Corfe Mullen	14
25	Creekmoor Ponds, Petersham Road	15
26	Leigh Common, Wimborne	15
27	Canford Church, Stour Meadows	15

continued overleaf...

WALK	LOCATION	PAGE
28	Eye Mead, Stour Valley Way	16
29	Fontmell and Melbury Estate	16
30	Win Green to Tollard Royal	16
31	Spetisbury to Keynston Mill	17
32	Blandford river walk	17
33	Bryanston river walk	17
34	Broadley Wood, nr Bryanston	20
35	Rawlsbury Camp Hill Fort	20
36	Ice Drove, Bulbarrow	21
37	Above Hilton Bottom	22
38	Shipstal, Arne	22
39	Hartland Moor	22
40	Middlebere Heath	23
41	Kingswood, Purbeck	24
42	Studland to 'Rest and be Thankful'	24
43	Corfe Castle 'Halves'	24
44	Peveril Point to Durlston, Victorian Trail	25
45	Kimmeridge Quarry to Ocean Seat	26
46	Kimmeridge to Lulworth Cove	26
47	Povington Hill to Tyneham circular walk	26
48	Tyneham Gwyle to Worbarrow Bay	27
49	Scratchy Bottom, Durdle Door	28
50	Near Bloxworth to Carey	28
51	Turners Puddle to Black Hill	29
52	Puddletown Forest	29
53	Greys Bridge Dorchester via Stinsford to Lower Bockhampton	29
54	Blue Bridge and The Walks, Dorchester	30
55	Five Marys, Chaldon	31
56	Portland Verne	31
57	Ferrybridge via coast to Chiswell	32
58	Pirates Cove, Wyke Regis Bridging Camp	32
59	Cerne Giant, Cerne Abbas	32
60	Eype Mouth to Golden Cap	33

'Things to do and places to visit' 33

INTRODUCTION

So many people told me how pleased they were to discover new places and dog-owning holidaymakers wrote to say their holidays had been 'made' by my walk books as they would never have found the walks on their own, that Bounty and I were persuaded to write this third (and final!) book.

Beforehand, I thought I knew the area pretty well, but I think the new walks in this book are even better than ever.

Many of the Wessex walkies are in Thomas Hardy country — particularly apt, as the famous Dorset writer owned a terrier named 'Wessex' — somewhat shaggier than my Bounty but otherwise rather similar in appearance. Not in character though, as *his* Wessex had a reputation for being thoroughly spoilt. Hardy's wife Florence bought him as a puppy in 1913. He lived for 13 years, bit everyone except the Hardys and T E Lawrence (of Arabia) and sat ON the tables at mealtimes demanding food!

Which leads me nicely to:

FOOD

The pubs and eating places shown are not necessarily starting points for the walks but are within reasonable distance by car and will all accommodate dogs inside, or in their gardens. A couple shown in previous books now have 'No dogs' signs due, I was told, to people complaining about their presence but please ask, as they say they will still admit them if current customers have no objection. I have yet to meet a badly behaved dog in any of the places I have visited — unlike some children!

CAUTION

The same warning again, DOGS ON LEAD when in fields with farm animals please. Farmers have the right to shoot loose dogs whether they are chasing stock or not. Also PLEASE keep your dog under control when you meet others. I speak with feeling, as my little Bounty is now frightened to use our one-time favourite walk at Luscombe Valley since he was set upon by a vicious dog. Lastly, which goes without saying really, please do not allow fouling of footpaths.

The information in this book was correct at the time of writing but I am sure you will appreciate it takes a long time to do all these walks, so please let me know if you come across any changes.

Once again, happy walkies!

WALK 1   LEPE COUNTRY PARK
DURATION   *approximately 1¼ hours leisurely walking*
STARTING POINT   *car park on the shore, or on the grassy headland*
FOOD   *Exbury Gardens Café, dogs outside only. The nearest pub is the Langley Tavern, dogs in conservatory only, but we found them 'not very dog-friendly'*

I suggest making the short climb on to the grassy headland where there is a good view plus picnic tables, rather than walk along the shingle. Follow the shoreline eastwards, with its close-up views of the Isle of Wight. In the distance ahead of you is the coast of Gosport and Portsmouth with Portsdown Hill on the horizon.

When you reach the two structures in the sea (which were part of the jetty for landing craft in World War Two and where the Mulberry Harbour was moored prior to being towed across the channel to Normandy for D-Day) the surface is grass-covered, making easier walking for little paws. There are rabbits here amongst the remains of strange concrete structures, also left over from WW2. This is Stanswood Bay where there are oyster beds, and the dark-looking headland across on the Isle of Wight is Egypt Point. Where the grass ends, a barbed wire fence marks the turning point of the walk and a sign declares it to be a North Solent National Nature Reserve of the Nature Conservancy Council. A pleasant, interesting walk.

WALK 2   BEAULIEU TO BUCKLERS HARD
DURATION   *approximately 2½ miles each way*
STARTING POINT   *Free car park, Beaulieu*
FOOD   *Old Bakehouse Tearooms, Beaulieu, dogs outside only. At Bucklers Hard, the Master Builder pub. Dogs requested to keep owners on lead!*

Go past the tearooms (which advertise LARGE cream teas) to a continuation of the footpath which then crosses a playing field. Lead restrictions apply for part of this walk. After passing between fenced fields you reach the North Solent Nature Reserve, 'a site of excellence' where a notice says dogs must be strictly controlled. We saw wild orchids in abundance here in June. There are glimpses of Beaulieu River on the left and houses on stilts in the woods to keep out floods. 150 yards past the first cottage an unmarked path goes off to the left. Follow this for better views alongside the river. After 1½ miles you rejoin the main footpath which you follow past a boatyard. The pretty little street of Bucklers Hard with its attendant ducks was very different in the 1740's when it was a thriving centre of ship-building. Many old oak ships of Nelson's time including the *Agamemnon* were built here.

See also THINGS TO DO for boat trips from Bucklers Hard.

WALK 3   IVY WOOD, NEAR BROCKENHURST
DURATION *flexible*
STARTING POINT *Ivy Wood car park*
FOOD *Royal Oak, Brockenhurst. Dogs allowed on lead*

From Brockenhurst Station turn right then sharp left into the B3055 Beaulieu road. Continue to the end where a sign indicates 'Turn right for Hatchett Pond'. Immediately on the right is the car park with a delightful forested area which follows a clear stream, where you may explore freely. Deer may be glimpsed hiding shyly between the trees and squirrels leap overhead in the branches. A lovely walk on a hot day if your dog enjoys a swim.

WALK 4   BOLTONS BENCH, LYNDHURST
DURATION *flexible*
STARTING POINT *Boltons Bench car park*
FOOD *New Forest Inn, Emery Down. Dogs on lead*

The car park is on the Southampton side of Lyndhurst, just on the outskirts of town. If the main car park in Lyndhurst is full which is often the case in summer, this is a good alternative and within easy walking distance. There are interesting walks to take from Boltons Bench on tracks that lead directly from the car park. The small church just over the hill has in its churchyard the grave of Alice Hargreaves, who was the inspiration for Alice in Wonderland.

WALK 5   JANESMOOR POND, STONEY CROSS
DURATION   *flexible*
STARTING POINT   *Stoney Cross disused airfield*
FOOD   *Royal Oak, Fritham drinks and crisps only, or New Forest Inn, Emery Down. Dogs on lead*

From the Linford – Boldrewood turning off the A31 you will find Stoney Cross airfield. Nearby is Longbeech campsite and just past this is Janesmoor Pond. Here you will be spoilt for choice with walks into the strangely named 'Kings Garn Gutter' inclosure ('Gutter' = New Forest word for brook or stream) or on the site of the old World War Two airfield where you could discover the remains of runway lights and hangar door tracking. When last there I saw a heron circling silently and landing in a pine tree. The pond is lovely for dogs to swim in when the weather is hot. There are toilets and a water tap not far from the water tower. This area is a dog's paradise and as there are miles of forest to explore, I suggest carrying an ordnance survey map!

WALK 6   STOCKBRIDGE DOWN
DURATION   *flexible*
STARTING POINT   *car park opposite Stockbridge Down*
FOOD   *Greyhound Inn, Dogs welcome. Vine Inn, dogs in large garden only. Both in Stockbridge.*

This walk begins 2 miles from Stockbridge on the A272 to Winchester. Park in one of the two car parks on the right and cross over to Stockbridge Down. This is a wonderful place! Scrub woodland and 160 acres of chalk downland rising to 158 m above sea level. There is Woolbury Hill, a simple single bank and ditch Iron Age hill fort dating from 500 BC and from the top of which are fantastic views. The springy turf has been nibbled low by countless rabbits and deer. Kestrels hover overhead and there is plenty of space for all.

WALK 7   MILLYFORD BRIDGE, NEAR LYNDHURST
DURATION   *flexible*
STARTING POINT   *Millyford Bridge car park*
FOOD   *New Forest Inn, Emery Down. Dogs on lead*

Just before Lyndhurst (coming from Bournemouth) turn left to Emery Down. By the New Forest Inn turn sharp left and about 1 mile on the right is Millyford Bridge. Take the gravel path which widens and follows the Highland Water stream for a while. There are wild roses by the path in summer and tall trees for shelter in windy, sunny or wet weather. If you continue to follow the main path, after about 1 mile of easy walking you come to Whisky Bridge where if you are lucky you may see deer. There are miles of tracks to follow in beautiful forest — but take care you don't get lost!

WALK 8   OAKLEY, NEW FOREST
DURATION *shortish walk*
STARTING POINT *Oakley car park*
FOOD *Old Station Tearooms, Holmesley. Dogs outside only, but a couple of tables under shelter. Closed Mondays.*

Turn left on the road before the Ornamental Drive coming from the direction of Bournemouth. Drive past a large area of woodland then some fields. After another half mile or so you will see Oakley car park on your right. Oakley Inclosure has lead restrictions but an interesting short walk outside the enclosure can be taken by following the fence, leaving it on your left. Can you identify the Kissing Tree? There are many fine trees here and one ancient oak must surely rival the famous Knightwood Oak at the start of the Ornamental Drive. The path is of soft, short grass and there are many interesting scents for your dog.

WALK 9   BURLEY, OPPOSITE THE GOLF COURSE
DURATION *flexible*
STARTING POINT *car park opposite Burley Golf Club*
FOOD *White Buck Inn. Dogs welcome on lead*

From the pretty but busy New Forest village of Burley go uphill past the Witches Coven shop. At the top of the hill park in the car park on the right (past the hotel car park). There are pleasant walks in many directions across open heathland dotted with New Forest ponies and cattle. At the bottom of the valley a pretty little stream runs through a grassy area with trees, but caution, this can be boggy at times. From the car park turn right in the direction of the A35 Bournemouth – Southampton road. After about a quarter of a mile on the left a signpost indicates the way to the White Buck Hotel — rather splendid — but dog-friendly nevertheless.

WALK 10 BROWNHILLS, HOLMESLEY NEW FOREST
DURATION *shortish walk*
STARTING POINT *near Old Station Tearooms on B3058*
FOOD *Old Station Tearooms. Dogs outside only but a couple of tables are under shelter. Closed Mondays.*

From Holmesley turn onto the B3058 towards Milford on Sea and a few metres on the left you will see Brownhills car park and picnic place. A wide, grassy ride stretches along the side of the Inclosure within sight of but a safe distance from the main Bournemouth to Southampton road. On our last visit we saw deer here. You can follow the outside of the Inclosure (dogs on leads inside) which dips downhill and with a bit of a struggle (it could be muddy) emerge near the Old Station Tearooms. This is a good place to take a break on a longer journey.

WALK 11   LONG MEADOW /BARTON COMMON, BARTON ON SEA
DURATION *flexible*
STARTING POINT *Long Meadow car park, Becton Lane*
FOOD *Beachcomber Café, Barton on Sea. Dogs welcome*

This is an open grassy area bisected by a small stream with a little wood, pleasant for a short walk but if you would like to extend it, cross over from the car park to a larger free car park just around the corner in Barton Common Road. Here you will find rough common ground alongside the golf course. Paths wind between gorse bushes and there is another little stream running through the lower ground.

WALK 12   DANES STREAM, MILFORD ON SEA
DURATION *approximately 1 hour's leisurely walk*
STARTING POINT *free car park opposite the Bay Tree Restaurant*
FOOD *Smugglers Inn. Dogs welcome*

Walk back towards Christchurch for a few metres and opposite Lucerne Road is the entrance to Milford on Sea Pleasure Grounds. The walk follows the banks of Danes Stream which meanders through pretty woods for approximately one mile. Fine properties can be glimpsed through the trees and many varieties of birds may be seen. About a third of the way along you come to a road but the path and stream continue on the other side until you reach a caravan park. Return by the same route but on the opposite side of the stream. The going can be muddy after heavy rain.

WALK 13   BLUE HAZE, RINGWOOD FOREST
DURATION *flexible*
STARTING POINT *150 metres past Blue Haze Pets Hotel*
FOOD *Alice Lisle Inn, Rockford. Dogs (but not children) welcome in Commoners bar.*

From Ringwood take the B3081 towards Alderholt and fork right after about 1 mile at Bakers Hanging. About 2½ miles further on along a pleasant road you will see the Blue Haze Pets Hotel on your left. About 50 metres past this on the left is a wide gateway where you may park considerately. There are miles of safe woodland tracks to explore with views across the heathland where some of the softly rustling pines have been cleared.

WALK 14   AVON VALLEY TRAMWAY
DURATION 1¾ *miles to River Stour, or flexible*
STARTING POINT *Lions Lane, Ashley Heath*
FOOD *Moors Valley Country Park Café, dogs outside only*

This walk follows the edge of Moors Valley Country Park past pinewoods. Pleasant enough with company, but if you are alone it is a bit of a long straight track for much of the way. Interesting insect life can be observed in this area. A much longer walk can be taken by turning left at the end of the Tramway through Watchmoor Wood and Moors Valley Country Park and — with care — returning to your starting point... but caution, the paths can look very similar and you could get lost. We did!

WALK 15   FISHERMANS BANK, STANPIT
DURATION *short stroll*
STARTING POINT *opposite 147 Stanpit*

Park in the road opposite 147 Stanpit and follow the harbour's edge around the back gardens of the houses. There are fine views across the estuary to Hengistbury Head and Christchurch harbour with its bird life, wind surfers and pleasure craft. Indeed there is always something to watch here whatever the season, while your dog can explore the water's edge and interesting scents. There are a couple of seats along the length of the walk which ends in a grassy stretch after passing a boatyard. Not very far, but very pleasant.

WALK 16   DRUITT GARDENS, CHRISTCHURCH
DURATION *short*
STARTING POINT *Wick Lane car park, Christchurch end*
FOOD *Kelly's Kitchen, High Street. Dogs allowed in pretty garden at rear or Ye Olde George Inn, well-behaved dogs on leads*

These are only small, wooded gardens between the market (Mondays only) and car park but they abound with squirrels and are a safe, off the lead walk if you are exploring this lovely old town. The gardens were given in 1946 by Charlotte Druitt for the use of the public. Ye Olde George Inn is of historical interest with boards displaying details of how *'Unfortunate prisoners were kept behind bars* (no, not THAT kind of bar!) *before being transported to Australia'*.

WALK 17   WOODLAND WALK, BOSCOMBE
DURATION *short*
STARTING POINT *Boscombe Overcliff Drive*

This walk begins from the clifftop behind the bowling green between Browning Avenue and Woodland Avenue and emerges into the shopping area of Christchurch Road through imposing large ornamental gates emblazoned with shields bearing Bournemouth's crest, *'Pulchritudo et Salubritas'* (Beauty and Health). This was originally the drive to Wentworth House, the summer residence of Lord Portman of Bryanston and built circa 1873. It was later to become Wentworth School. A pleasant, sheltered walk through rhododendrons, chestnuts, oaks and hollies which at certain times abound with squirrels. The surface is tarmac so with the trees overhead is particularly good in wet, windy or even hot weather.

WALK 18   MUSCLIFFE ARBORETUM
DURATION *flexible*
STARTING POINT *Muscliffe Lane, opposite Aragon Way*

Continue down Muscliffe Lane for a short distance to where the road narrows, and on the left, set back a little is the gateway leading to the Arboretum. On the far side of the open space which you will soon reach is Shelley Lodge once owned by the poet's younger brother. A safe, off the lead walk where you can circle the Arboretum with its widely spaced specimen trees or go straight on to the river and follow the bank where I have seen a kingfisher. On the opposite side of Muscliffe Lane you may have noticed a path leading off to the right, also safe off the lead and which meanders past playing fields, eventually emerging into The Broadway.

WALK 19   PARKSTONE 'LAKES'
DURATION *shortish*
STARTING POINT *Mill Lane, entrance to Baden Powell & St Peter School*
From Mill Lane, head east from the school entrance along a footpath. After about 100 metres you will reach a five-bar gate. Go through and follow the path. The bank alongside was part of the old pottery boundary which used to be on the site. Cross over Conifer Road where the footpath continues until it reaches a pretty pond with ducks, somewhat loftily known as 'Parkstone lakes'.

WALK 20   CONSTITUTION HILL VIEWPOINT, PARKSTONE
DURATION *short*
STARTING POINT *car park at View Point*
FOOD *teas and sandwiches at kiosk in car park*
Outstanding panoramic views of Poole harbour, town and the Purbeck hills. Pinewoods cover the slopes and there are many paths to explore. A memorial at the viewpoint is dedicated to an 18 year old Royal Marine from Poole who lost his life in the Falklands war. Members of the Special Boat Squad can be seen at exercise in the harbour at times.

WALK 21   BAITER TO POOLE QUAY
DURATION *short*
STARTING POINT *free car park (furthest) at Baiter*
Take the tarmac path which follows the shoreline and is safe off the lead. A short walk with fine views of Poole harbour, the Purbeck hills and shipping entering and leaving the port. (See list of *'Things to do'* for boat trips from the quay). On your way you will pass the old Lifeboat Station which is now a museum and well worth a visit. Admission free.

WALK 22   PARRS PLANTATION, POOLE
DURATION *short*
STARTING POINT *Dale Valley Road, by St Edwards School entrance*
One of many plantations planted on the heath in the 19th century and given a Forestry Centre of Excellence Award in 1992, this is a small piece of mixed woodland surrounded by a built up area and alongside (but safely fenced from) the busy Old Wareham Road dual carriageway. The way into the Plantation is on the left of the school entrance gates. There are several paths to explore with pines, a small bog area and heather. The site was originally twice the present size but in the 1930s was farmed and then St Edwards School was built on part of the land.

WALK 23 KNIGHTON HEATH, BY GOLF COURSE
DURATION *flexible*
STARTING POINT *Francis Avenue, Alderney*
From the roundabout at the junction of Wallisdown Road and Ringwood Road turn off to Francis Avenue and park at the far end. I make no apologies for including part of Canford Heath (see *Wessex Walkies*) again as this walk has a different starting point and the area covered is large enough to give a varied choice of paths. Follow the finger-board to Canford Heath along the tarmac path to the end alongside the waterworks. Bear right around the golf course (not through, although there is a footpath there but also hazards from flying golf balls!) where you will find plenty of paths to choose from with heather-clad views towards Wimborne, Poole and Purbeck. This heathland is home for rare Dartford Warblers, smooth snakes and sand lizards.

WALK 24 HAPPY BOTTOM , CORFE MULLEN
DURATION *flexible*
STARTING POINT *Higher Blandford Road, Corfe Mullen*
FOOD *Lambs Green Inn. Dogs outside only but some tables under shelter*
Start from the dip in Higher Blandford Road past Corfe Hills School leaving the school on your left. The path is a continuation of the Roman road from Upton but Corfe Mullen is a good starting place, as nearer Poole the road is built up. The footpath is on the right and leads to Rushcombe Bottom, an area of rough heath. Make sure you keep left on the Roman road at a three-way signpost, leaving Barrow Hill on your right. Cross Merley Park Road to FP No. 6. Continue along through oaks, hazels and hollies and over a wooden bridge followed by more woodland. At the end of a gravel path is the tiny hamlet of Happy Bottom. Here, if you require sustenance you may continue along the road until Lambs Green Lane joins from the left. A little way along to the left is the Lambs Green Inn where, unasked, a waiter brought Bounty my dog a bowl of water. If you want a circular walk, from Happy Bottom take the footpath to Ashington Lane then back to Merley Park Road. Turn right opposite the old corrugated iron church into a lane then follow a footpath past Heatherwood Nurseries. Follow this until you reach the three directional signpost which you passed on your outward journey and make your way back via Rushcombe Bottom. Rather more complicated than my usual instructions — so please don't get lost!

WALK 25   CREEKMOOR PONDS
DURATION *shortish*
STARTING POINT *Petersham Road, Creekmoor or limited space on site*
Old clay workings have been transformed into a pretty wildlife reserve, a far cry from when a little steam engine used to chuff along with its loads of clay. Water lilies bloom in season and if you follow the tarmac path it will take you right around the ponds, finally emerging further down Petersham Road. Deep water is surrounded by trees with a variety of birds. Swallows and swifts swoop over the surface in summer catching insects, while swans glide majestically over the still surface and rear their cygnets in safety.

WALK 26   LEIGH COMMON, WIMBORNE
DURATION *short*
STARTING POINT *B 3073 Leigh Road, Wimborne*
Just past the Sir Winston Churchill pub looking towards Wimborne a rough lane leads to Leigh Common. A scattering of cottages face the Common so please park considerately so access is not blocked. Several paths wind in and out of the trees to give a pleasant, sheltered walk.

WALK 27   CANFORD CHURCH, STOUR MEADOWS
DURATION *flexible*
STARTING POINT *adjacent to Canford church by the entrance to Canford School*
FOOD *Lambs Green Inn. Dogs outside only but some tables under cover*
There are several choices of walks: left along the shady old estate carriage road to Wimborne or the footpath through the white barrier which bears right across a narrow suspension footbridge which will take you along the riverbank to the left, a pleasant stroll. A longer walk can be taken by turning right after crossing the bridge where you have the choice of paths to Stapehill or Leigh Road, Wimborne. There are fine views of Canford School and John O' Gaunt's Kitchen from the riverbank. The school was the home of Lord and Lady Wimborne until 1922. John O'Gaunt's Kitchen dates back to the Norman Conquest, the only part remaining from that period. In 1198 William Longspee, one of the founders of Salisbury Cathedral lived there. The church, dating from Saxon times is worth a visit. On a board hanging on the tower wall are the following lines:

> 'It is not good to hear Men Wrangle
> It is not good to hear Bells Jangle
> For there is no Music Play'd or Sung
> To be compared to Bells well Rung'

WALK 28   EYE MEAD, STOUR VALLEY WAY
DURATION *flexible*
STARTING PLACE *Eye Mead (NT) car park*
FOOD *Vine Inn, Pamphill. Tiny — but dogs welcome. Large garden*

From Wimborne Cottage Hospital drive past Wimborne Football Ground. Turn left past a cottage in the trees to a ford, with parking places in a field. There was a ford here in Roman times. If you cross over the footbridge a sign requests 'dogs on lead' but follow upstream without crossing over and the request is 'dogs under control'. The path is lined with sheep wire so quite safe. This is a lovely summer walk as your dog can swim in clear water. At a wood the path bears right. Take this, as straight on leads nowhere. If you visit the Vine Inn you will discover a minuscule, friendly pub. Lunchtime snacks only. The pub is small but the garden large and dogs are welcome anywhere.

WALK 29   FONTMELL AND MELBURY ESTATE
DURATION *flexible*
STARTING POINT *Ashmore/Compton Abbas airfield road*
FOOD *Rising Sun Inn, A30 nr Donhead. Dogs allowed? 'Of course!'*

From Win Green take the Ashmore/Compton Abbas airfield road. Approximately 200 metres on the right is a stile and map board. Follow the signs to Melbury Beacon or Compton Down by paths which extend along a deep valley with rolling hills above. This is National Trust land. An alternative approach is from the high Blandford/Shaftesbury road. Turn by Compton Abbas airfield leaving it on your left. Where the road forks turn left towards Donhead and you will find the walk's starting place on the left.

WALK 30   WIN GREEN TO TOLLARD ROYAL
DURATION *flexible*
STARTING POINT *Win Green car park*
FOOD *Rising Sun Inn, A30 nr Donhead. Dogs allowed? 'Of course!' or King John Inn, Tollard Royal. Dogs on lead permitted.*

Win Green is reached from the B3081 Sixpenny Handley to Shaftesbury road where a sign indicates, 'Byway to Win Green'. From the car park follow the fence on the right until you reach a stile with a yellow marker in the corner of the field. Climb over and head left down the hill which is steep in parts and not for the faint-hearted! The going is through rough scrubby ground popular with dogs. Before you is the most beautiful valley surrounded by hills rich with colour in autumn, a glory to behold. In the distance is the New Forest. A sign asks that your dog be on a lead whilst going through a wood as pheasants and deer abound. After a short distance you emerge along the valley bottom and follow the Wessex Ridgeway signs as far as Tollard Royal. According to folklore there is a Quakers Burial ground with sloping headstones in the vicinity of Win Green but I have yet to find it. Perhaps you will be more fortunate. To extend the walk, you could lunch at the King John Inn, Tollard Royal. After looking around this tiny pretty village in its hidden valley you could take the track back uphill past the village pond, again marked 'Byway to Win Green'. This is a slightly longer walk than the outward journey but you will be on the crest of the hills giving glorious, different views from the beautiful valley ones of the first walk. This whole area is delightful.

WALK 31 SPETISBURY TO KEYNSTON MILL
DURATION *short*
STARTING POINT *opposite the village school, Spetisbury*
FOOD *Keynston Mill, dogs outside only*

Opposite the village school a footpath meanders off across fields to a narrow footbridge over the River Stour. On the far side a little way up the lane is Keynston Mill Shop, Café and PYO fruit and veg — so come prepared! Return by the same path.

WALK 32 BLANDFORD RIVER
DURATION *short*
STARTING POINT *main car park, Blandford*
FOOD *Greyhound Inn, just off car park. Dogs on lead welcome*

This is a short walk on a grassy area between the main car park on the Poole – Blandford road behind Safeways and the river, which could easily be missed as it is on a lower level and out of sight of the car park. There is a weir with ducks for interest and the grassy area extends between two arms of the River Stour. A pleasant, off the lead walk if you have been exploring or shopping in the old Georgian town of Blandford. There are toilets and a Tourist Information Centre at the entrance to the car park.

WALK 33 BRYANSTON RIVER WALK
DURATION   *2 miles return*
STARTING POINT *Blandford main car park*
FOOD *Crown Hotel, Blandford. Dogs welcome*

Go through the main gates to Bryanston School. Although a notice says 'Private grounds' there is a public right of way through the gates to the right. Follow the river bank along a pleasant, shady path. There are fine trees, many of which have their roots exposed where they cling to the steep hillside. At the far end you reach an old chapel. Pause a while to contemplate this peaceful part of Dorset before returning the way you came.

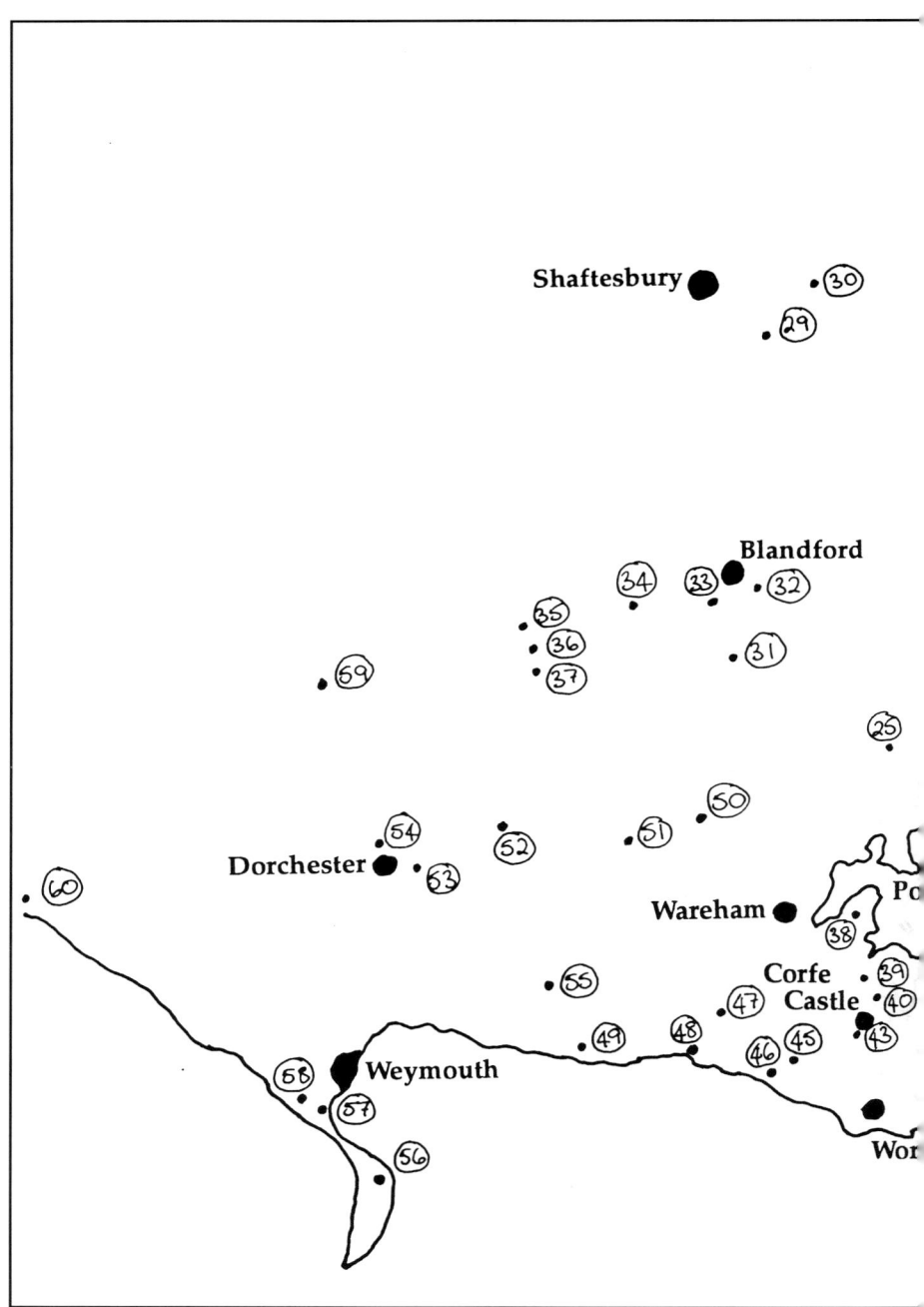

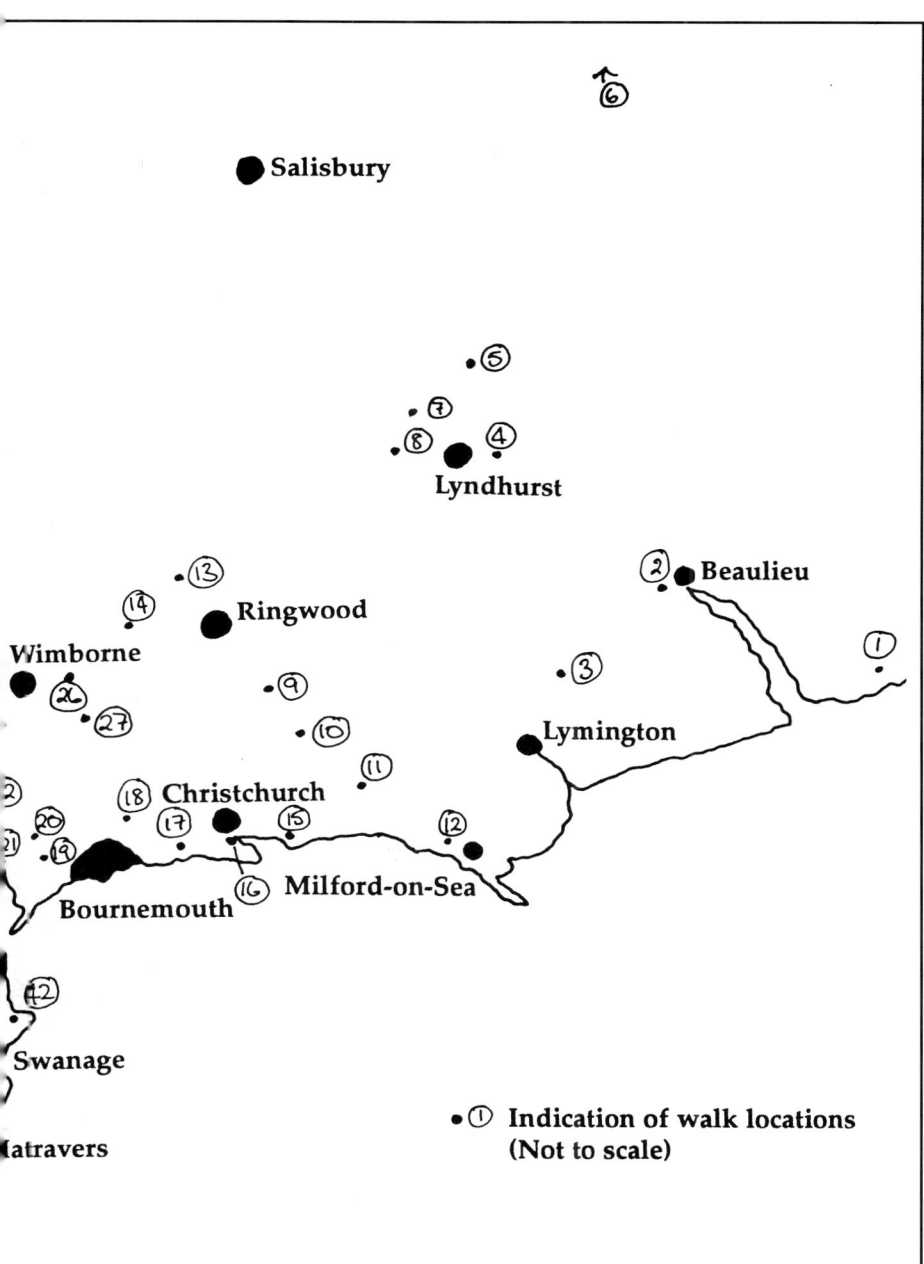

WALK 34 BROADLEY WOOD
DURATION *flexible*
STARTING POINT *entrance to Broadley Wood*
FOOD *Crown Hotel, or Greyhound Inn Blandford. Dogs welcome*

From Blandford, drive past the main entrance to Bryanston School and turn 2nd right, signposted 'Winterborne Stickland'. Drive on this road for about 1 mile. Past Green Acres Caravan Park the road bears right and a few metres around the bend on the right hand side is the entrance to Broadley Wood. A Forestry Commission sign requests that access to the gateway is kept clear. Follow the blue bridleway markers along a dry, gravel track into the woods. You will discover several paths and tracks leading off for you to explore in this lovely deciduous woodland. I have seen pheasants, woodpeckers and other wildlife on my walks there.

WALK 35 RAWLSBURY CAMP HILL FORT
DURATION *flexible*
STARTING POINT *Bulbarrow*
FOOD *Fox Inn, Anstey. Dogs outside only*

From Blandford take the A354 westwards and just past the entrance to Bryanston School turn right to Winterborne Stickland. Once there, follow the signs to Bulbarrow. From there head downhill towards Stoke Wake for ¼ mile. These directions may sound complicated but when you arrive the views will be well worth the trouble. Park on the left where there is a gate with a

Wessex Ridgeway sign, and another, 'Rawlsbury Hill Fort'. There is only room for two cars at most so do park with care. The path extends in both directions for you to explore at will. If the day is clear your efforts will be rewarded with superb views across to the Dorset Gap and Nettlecombe Tout. Rawlsbury was constructed in the Iron Age as a hill fort and in this case the distances between ditch and bank were increased to enclose largish areas of ground. You will find no better views than these for miles.

WALK 36   THE ICE DROVE, BULBARROW
DURATION *flexible*
STARTING POINT *Bulbarrow*
FOOD *The Fox, Anstey, or Hambro Arms, Milton Abbas. Dogs outside only at both.*

From Bulbarrow (see Walk 35 for directions) take the road to Anstey and Hilton. After about ¼ mile you pass the entrance to Bulbarrow Farm. Park just past this on the left under a large oak on the grass verge. The Ice Drove is a double-hedged ancient trackway giving superb views across the lush Dorset valleys and gorse-covered chalk downland. It leads to the Greenhill Nature Reserve where deer tracks and rabbits can be seen as well as wild flowers and insects which make this countryside so special. A bridleway continues 1¾ miles to Hilton and Milton Abbas.

WALK 37   ABOVE HILTON BOTTOM
DURATION *shortish*
STARTING POINT *approx ½ mile further downhill from Ice Drove (Walk 36)*
FOOD *The Fox, Anstey or Hambro Arms Milton Abbas. Dogs outside only at both.*

Approximately ½ mile further down the hill from the Ice Drove starting point you will see a gateway with a small pull-in on the left. A little map is attached to a gatepost and yellow and blue markings indicate a footpath and bridleway. A notice states that this is not a permanent right of way but the landowner has opened it to the public under the Countryside Scheme. This is being developed by the Countryside Commission which offers the farmer incentives in exchange for a 10 year management agreement making valued landscapes available for the public to enjoy. There are superb views once again overlooking Hilton and the valley below as far as Studland cliffs and Ballard Down in Purbeck in one direction and possibly even the Mendip Hills on a very clear day in the other. In the field is a small but ancient ash tree by a water trough. A lovely, inspiring walk.

WALK 38   SHIPSTAL, ARNE
DURATION *flexible*
STARTING POINT *RSPB car park, Arne*
FOOD *Marblers Café or Greyhound Inn, Corfe Castle. Dogs on lead welcome.*

From the RSPB car park (where there are toilets) continue along the road and follow the signposts to Shipstal Point. The rough, fenced track leads across farmland, through woods and eventually to the harbour shore where there are fine views across the water to the islands and Purbeck hills. Follow the shoreline to the right which will bring you back through the woods. Pottery was made and exported from here in the Iron Age and Romano/British era. As the path traverses an RSPB reserve please keep your dog under control to avoid disturbing wildlife. Dogs are permitted off the lead on the beach but on some of the paths leading from the main track you are requested to put them on leads. A very pleasant walk.

WALK 39   HARTLAND MOOR
DURATION *approximately 1 hour round trip*
STARTING POINT *opposite Middlebere Farm entrance*
FOOD *Marblers Café or Greyhound Inn, Corfe Castle. Dogs on lead welcome.*

From the Wareham/Arne road turn right towards Corfe Castle. Continue for about 1 mile where on the right you will see a sign, 'Hartland Moor'. Park on the verge opposite Middlebere Farm entrance and go through a five

bar gate along a grassy track bordered by sloes and hawthorn which was the old clay workings tramway. Rare Dartford Warblers, sand lizards, deer, marsh gentians and a great diversity of insects may be seen if you are lucky. There are wide expanses of heath and bog with hardly a sign of habitation for miles and this must be one of the most evocative landscapes left in Dorset. The walk extends as far as a grove of trees surrounding a boggy emergency water supply and then you must retrace your steps. This walk is usually dry underfoot all the way.

WALK 40 MIDDLEBERE HEATH
DURATION *flexible*
STARTING POINT *as Walk 39*
FOOD *Marblers Café or Greyhound Inn, Corfe Castle. Dogs on lead welcome.*

Park opposite Hartland Moor sign on Arne/Corfe Castle road or from Wytch Roundabout near Corfe Castle, take the Arne road which also leads there. A sign reads, 'Lowland Heath Restoration Study Project' and this is where your walk begins. An open, grassy expanse with fabulous views to Pcole harbour lies before you, the only sign of civilisation being the ruins of Corfe Castle. Rolling uninhabited heathland stretches around with the study area enclosed in the middle. Red Devon cattle have recently been introduced by the National Trust from Kingston Lacy to graze the rough grass. I think you will enjoy this one.

WALK 41   KINGSWOOD, PURBECK
DURATION *flexible*
STARTING POINT *viewpoint on Corfe Castle to Swanage minor road*
FOOD *Manor House Hotel, Studland. Dogs outside only but lovely setting, or Bankes Arms, Studland. Dogs allowed.*

From the Viewpoint layby near Swanage golf club, 200/300 metres eastwards you will see a bridleway with a fingerboard, 'Nine Barrow Down 1 mile'. Follow this track for fabulous views across Poole harbour, Shell Bay and the Bournemouth coastline. From the top of the Downs even more panoramas stretch in all directions. This 'downs and woodland' walk is well recommended.

WALK 42   STUDLAND TO 'REST AND BE THANKFUL'
DURATION *flexible*
STARTING POINT *National Trust car park by Bankes Arms, Studland*
FOOD *Manor House Studland, dogs outside only or Bankes Arms Studland, dogs allowed.*

From the car park walk towards the old Norman church. Take a closer look at the stone cross on the corner, modern on a Saxon base. Dated 1976 it is inscribed, 'Spaceship Earth'. The bridleway goes past Manor Farm and up the hill towards Swanage. Stop to get your breath and look back at the view — Shell Bay, Poole harbour, Bournemouth cliffs and the Isle of Wight in the distance. The tarmac peters out eventually and you continue up the hill by way of a footpath. 'Rest and be Thankful' is a stone seat on top of the hill and from it on a clear day you can see as far as Arthur's Tower at Stourhead in Wiltshire. Continue on to Swanage or turn left and return via Old Harry Rocks, about 2½ miles.

WALK 43   CORFE CASTLE 'HALVES'
DURATION *flexible*
STARTING POINT *West Street car park, Corfe Castle*
FOOD *Marblers Café or Greyhound Inn. Well behaved dogs on leads welcome.*

From the car park (free off season) head back towards the castle. On your right between the old fashioned butcher's and Marblers Café and Gift Shop is a footpath marked with the yellow arrow symbol, adjacent to 19 West Street. Follow this and you emerge into the 'Halves' or 'Hawes' as they were called in the 16th century. There are four safe, off the lead fields to explore which rarely contain stock. A shortish walk can be taken by circling the fields or a longer one by following the main footpath. It passes behind and to the left of houses at the end of the fourth field, on the gate of which has been carved the inscription, 'George Snow passed this way' and crosses a cul-de-

sac, emerging into 350 acres of Corfe Common, truly a delight. Little brooks flow along the valley and in their season wild orchids, butterflies and blackberries are plentiful. Commoners still graze their animals here as they have for hundreds of years. One of our favourite walks.

WALK 44 PEVERIL POINT TO DURLSTON, VICTORIAN TRAIL
DURATION *flexible*
STARTING POINT *car park on Peveril Point, Swanage*
FOOD *Durlston Castle, 2 and 4 legged walkers welcome!*
From the car park head uphill to the cliff's edge. There is rather rough access to the rocky beach at Peveril Point end but this walk follows the cliff-top. Take care as dogs have fallen over here. The way is clearly marked and after the first hill dips down into a pleasantly wooded area, ideal in hot, wet or windy weather. The path emerges by Durlston Castle with its dog-friendly bar and Café with excellent food. On a hot summer's day it is a treat to sit outside in the garden with views of the sea and coast. Cross-channel ferries sail past and yachts and fishing craft can be seen. A beautiful sight. We often say, 'Who would wish to be anywhere else. Why go abroad when we have this on our doorstep?' If you feel like a longer walk, all of Durlston Country Park is there for your delight.

WALK 45 KIMMERIDGE QUARRY TO OCEAN SEAT
(NOTE — ONLY WHEN THE ARMY GUNNERY RANGES ARE OPEN)
Range walks usually open at the following times: one week at Easter; one week at Spring Bank Holiday; last week in July to 2nd week in Sept (inclusive); 2 weeks at Christmas; most weekends
DURATION *approximately 1 mile each way*
STARTING POINT *Disused quarry before Smedmore*
FOOD *Seven Taps, Kimmeridge. Dogs outside only.*

Park (free) in the disused quarry on the left just before the turning to Smedmore. Cross the road going back uphill where you will see two footpath signs. Follow the higher one which directs you along the scarp of the hill above Kimmeridge Church (which has the grave of an Excise man killed by smugglers in the churchyard). At roughly the halfway mark you pass Ridgeway Gate then continue along a rough track to Ocean Seat, a rough, drystone refuge and fine viewpoint. Extensive panoramas abound in all directions — but it can be breezy here, so come prepared! After enjoying the views, return by the same paths.

WALK 46 KIMMERIDGE TO LULWORTH COVE
(ONLY WHEN ARMY RANGE WALKS OPEN — see WALK 45)
DURATION *allow half a day*
STARTING POINT *Kimmeridge Bay car park*
FOOD *Lulworth Heritage Car Park Café. Dogs outside only but some seats under cover.*

From Kimmeridge car park (charge in summer) walk westwards past the 'nodding donkeys' of the oil well. The South Western Coastal Path discloses superb scenery passing Broad Bench, Tyneham Cap, the contorted Gad Cliff and on to Worbarrow Bay. From here there is one of the steepest paths in Purbeck which climbs up to Flowers Barrow, an Iron Age hill fort which has partially crumbled into the sea and where many people over the centuries have reported seeing a ghostly Roman Legion marching! The scenery is breathtaking as you descend to the tiny bay of Arish Mell then another stiff climb up Bindon Hill. Below you are the Mupe rocks and, if you sidetrack down a flight of steps you will see the Fossil Forest, petrified tree stumps from millions of years ago. You may be directed inland from here as on my last visit the cliff path was in a dangerous condition. Lulworth Cove is beautiful, almost circular and a holidaymakers Mecca in summer.

WALK 47 POVINGTON HILL CIRCULAR WALK VIA TYNEHAM
(ONLY WHEN ARMY RANGE WALKS OPEN — see WALK 45)
DURATION *approximately 5 miles*

STARTING POINT *Povington Hill car park, Purbeck*
FOOD *Greyhound Inn, Corfe Castle. Dogs on lead welcome.*
A circular walk with to my mind unsurpassed scenery anywhere else in Wessex. Head westward from the car park along the crest of the Purbecks. The views are superb as you approach Flowers Barrow with the deserted village of Tyneham in the valley below and Worbarrow Tout rising from the bay ahead. The path climbs steeply down to the sea and can be slippery when wet, so take care. Once you reach the beach you may notice sands in the cliff which rival the famous coloured sands of Alum Bay in the Isle of Wight. In fact this is the westerly end of the same strata. In Tyneham Church, now an Information Centre there are leaflets describing the village as it was before being taken over by the MOD in 1943 and well worth investigating. Take the wide gravel track behind the church which will lead you uphill and eventually back to Whitehill picnic place and Povington Hill car park.

WALK 48 TYNEHAM GWYLE TO WORBARROW BAY
(ONLY WHEN ARMY RANGE WALKS OPEN — see WALK 45)
DURATION *approximately ½ hour each way*
STARTING POINT *Tyneham car park*
FOOD *Greyhound Inn, Corfe Castle. Dogs allowed on lead.*
From the large car park in Tyneham village (which was evacuated by the MOD in 1943 to enable the area to be used as an army training ground) take

the waymarked footpath to the seashore with wonderful views of the Purbeck hills and this 'lost' valley along the way. Worbarrow Tout's conical shape appears on your left and there is a footpath to the top if you have the energy! Just to the left of the Tout is the tiny Pondfield Cove with its pebbly beach. At Worbarrow Bay a little stream runs into the sea if your dog needs a drink. On your return to Tyneham village go past Post Office Row with its old fashioned telephone kiosk and you will find leaflets describing the village's history in the little church which dates from the 13th century and is now a museum and Information Centre.

WALK 49 SCRATCHY BOTTOM , DURDLE DOOR
DURATION *allow a couple of hours or more*
STARTING POINT *grass verge near entrance to Durdle Door Caravan Park*
FOOD *Durdle Door Caravan Park Café. Dogs allowed outside.*
From Lulworth take the road to Winfrith and Durdle Door and park as above. Follow the footpath past Newlands Farm and when it forks, bear left downhill along the valley. This is Scratchy Bottom and much more pleasant than its name suggests! You will find rolling chalk downland with sea views when you reach the coast. If you follow the coastal path to the left for a little way you will see Durdle Door, that strange formation of rocks which to me resembles a huge dragon drinking. Take care of your dog here though as the cliffs are very steep. You can continue back uphill (steepish!) through the Caravan Camp or go back to Scratchy Bottom and complete the circuit in the other direction. If you choose the former, in summer there is a Café there with pleasant tables outside. If you are wondering what the large, strange fossil-looking shell set in a wall is which you may have seen on your walk, it is a memorial to a member of the Powys family.

WALK 50 NEAR BLOXWORTH TO CAREY
DURATION *3 miles*
STARTING POINT *Bridle path off A35 nr Bloxworth on Poole — Bere Regis road*
FOOD *The Cock and Bottle, Morden. Dogs welcome.*
On your left going towards Bere Regis you will see a fingerboard, 'Carey 3 miles'. The track goes through woodland and crosses a stream by shallow ford or footbridge, the choice is yours. Follow the blue bridleway signs through pinewoods. You can sidetrack to Woolsbarrow Iron Age hill fort if you want to vary the walk, which will give you good views of the surrounding countryside.

WALK 51   TURNERS PUDDLE TO BLACK HILL
DURATION *flexible*
STARTING POINT *Turners Puddle, near the church*
FOOD *Royal Oak, Bere Regis. Dogs on lead welcome.*

Park near the Church of the Holy Trinity, parts of which date from 1500 although the roof is of weathered asbestos. The bridle path pointing uphill by the farm will lead you to Black Hill, over 200 feet above sea level. There are fine views from the ridge and many tracks to explore and if you are lucky you may see deer. You can detour before reaching Black Hill by following the footpath signs to the right across fields as you head uphill. This will take you to the top by a different route. Another alternative is to keep on the wide gravel track, ignoring any turnings. It emerges at the hamlet of Shitterton in the valley. Go past the cottages along the road and turn right past the bridge. You could lunch at the Royal Oak in Bere Regis and return by the same way.

WALK 52   PUDDLETOWN FOREST
DURATION *flexible*
STARTING POINT *grassy verge by Puddletown Forest*
FOOD *Blue Vinney, Puddletown. Dogs permitted on lead.*

From Puddletown drive up New Road past St Mary's School for about 1 mile. When the road turns sharp left you will find various lay-bys on either side of the road for the next mile. Any of these give access to Puddletown Forest which is on the right. There are miles of paths to follow through tall trees and open heathland. The track of the old Roman road from Badbury Rings to Dorchester crosses the forest and rumour has it that the ghost of a Centurion has been seen here. On the far side of the forest is Thomas Hardy's cottage where the famous Dorset author was born and where he wrote *Under the Greenwood Tree*.

WALK 53   GREYS BRIDGE DORCHESTER TO LOWER BOCKHAMPTON
DURATION *flexible*
STARTING POINT *A35 layby just before turn to B3143*
FOOD *Cornwall Hotel, Dorchester. Dogs very welcome.*

Cross over the road and about 100 metres or so on the left, just before Greys Bridge (which was the scene of the tragic end of Henchard in Thomas Hardy's *Mayor of Casterbridge*) a footpath follows the river bank. At first it may appear uninteresting, but after passing a pretty thatched residence, 'Three Bears Cottage' on the left (where I have seen a kingfisher) there is a detour to Stinsford Church. Thomas Hardy, the famous Dorset author was born in the parish of Stinsford at Higher Bockhampton on 2nd June 1840 and baptised

in this church with which his family had connections. On his death and against his wishes his body was buried in Westminster Abbey but his heart was removed and lies buried here in Stinsford Churchyard in his beloved Dorset. Return to the streamside walk which passes behind the lovely old house of Kingston Maurward, now an agricultural college. This walk is at its best in autumn, winter or early spring when the pretty, clear gravel stream is not hidden by undergrowth. The walk can be extended by continuing on to Norris Mill after you reach Lower Bockhampton.

WALK 54 BLUE BRIDGE AND THE WALKS, DORCHESTER
DURATION *flexible*
STARTING POINT *Top-o-Town car park, Dorchester*
FOOD *Cornwall Hotel, Alexander Road, Dorchester. Dogs most welcome.*
From Top-o-Town car park cross over the road towards County Hall by the life-sized statue of Thomas Hardy. A tree-lined footpath follows Colliton Walk with its steep grassy banks sloping down to the road below. These banks were part of the old Roman wall around Dorchester. Continue around the corner, perhaps pausing to view the site of Colliton Park Town House, the remains of a Roman Villa. This is signposted through the wall on your right (no admission charge). Follow the path down to the road opposite the pretty thatched Hangman's Cottage, mentioned in Hardy's *Mayor of*

Casterbridge. Signposts indicate Blue Bridge, a short distance away along a narrow footpath. This is a favourite spot in hot weather as there is a clear, gravel-bottomed ford by the bridge in which dogs love to romp. To extend the walk, retrace your steps and follow the path along the other arm of the river which follows the Frome Path. The kink in the path and narrowing of the stream marks the site of the old Friary Mill, long since disappeared. The walk eventually emerges into Dorchester High Street alongside the White Hart (no dogs).

WALK 55 FIVE MARY'S, CHALDON
DURATION *flexible*
STARTING POINT *crest of hill above Sailor's Return, Chaldon*
FOOD *Sailor's Return, Chaldon. Well-behaved dogs on lead in public bar and garden.*

From the A352 Wareham to Winfrith road take the turning to West Chaldon. At the crest of the hill is a grassy verge where you may park. A signpost indicates, '5 Mary's ¼ mile, Winfrith 1 mile' along a grassy or hard earth track. There are superb views in all directions. A longer walk may be taken by crossing the road at the start of this walk and heading along the grassy path to White Horse Hill, 4½ miles away along the ridge although the path which follows a hedgerow after going through a gate towards Lords Barrow is not very clearly defined, so care is needed.

WALK 56 THE VERNE, PORTLAND
DURATION *flexible*
STARTING POINT *car park at the top of the hill at Portland*
FOOD *Little Ship, Chiswell. Dogs allowed in public bar.*

Park in the car park at the top of the hill on the left in Verne Hill Road. Walk to the far end and follow the waymarked footpath along the contours of The Verne. Go through a gate which says, 'MOD Property. Please keep gate closed, cattle grazing'. There are views over Lyme Bay, Portland Harbour, Wyke Regis, Weymouth and the Dorset coastline. You will pass a beautifully sited Naval cemetery on your right. On top of the cliff is a large 'golf ball' poised as if ready to fall. The path finally stops at another MOD gate. Helicopters and warships could once be seen here but in 1995 the Naval Dockyard closed.

WALK 57   FERRYBRIDGE VIA COAST TO CHISWELL
DURATION *approximately 2 miles*
STARTING POINT *Ferrybridge car park (charge)*
FOOD *Little Ship, Chiswell. Dogs allowed in public bar.*
From the car park (where there are toilets) cross the road to the harbour side and head towards Portland along the grassy edge of the shore. A railway line once ran along here and you may see evidence of this. A pleasant walk with views of sailing boats , windsurfers, Portland harbour and the Dorset coastline.

WALK 58   PIRATES COVE, WYKE REGIS BRIDGING CAMP
DURATION *approximately 1 mile each way*
STARTING POINT *road alongside Bridging Camp*
FOOD *Old Castle Inn, Castle Cove. Dogs allowed in Clearmount Road bar.*
From Wyke Regis Bridging Camp which is signposted from the B3157 Wyke to Abbotsbury road, take the footpath leading off to the left. In front of you beyond the Fleet is the Chesil Bank which extends some 15 miles to West Bay. The pebbles have been naturally graded by the action of the waves, the largest being found at Portland and decreasing to pea size at the far end. The footpath crosses a field then follows the low cliff along the Fleet to Pirates Cove.

WALK 59   CERNE GIANT, CERNE ABBAS
DURATION *flexible*
STARTING POINT *Cerne Abbas village*
FOOD *Royal Oak, Cerne Abbas. Dogs? 'No problem!'*
Park in the village and walk past the church and old Tudor houses towards the abbey ruins which date from the 14th century. A footpath crosses fields from the right-angle of the wall and leads uphill through pleasant woods to the 180 foot long figure of the Giant. His origins are lost in the mists of time but he is very ancient and undoubtedly a fertility symbol. You can follow sheep tracks below and above his imposing form but the Giant himself is fenced off to prevent erosion.

WALK 60 EYPE MOUTH TO GOLDEN CAP
DURATION *approximately 4 miles each way*
STARTING POINT *Eype Mouth car park*
FOOD *The New Inn, Eype. Dogs welcome.*

From the beach there is a spectacular switchback walk along the National Trust cliff-top to Golden Cap. Eype Mouth is a collection of wooden chalets, a World War Two pillbox, car park and fishing boats. Head west towards Seatown and you will soon discover a beautiful grassy valley some 100 feet above the beach which is aglow with sea pinks in late spring. Thorncombe Beacon is next with a climb to about 450 feet through wild, gorse country. Down again over Doghouse Hill followed by the steep descent of Ridge Cliff. The next landmark is Seatown, a small collection of wooden chalets, a thatched cottage and a pub. After a breather perhaps, ascend the Wear Cliffs and you will have your goal in sight. At 617 feet Golden Cap is the highest cliff in Southern England and it is well worth the effort on a clear day to see the splendid views across Lyme Bay and Marshwood Vale.

THINGS TO DO AND PLACES TO VISIT

I always like to take my dog with me, and have discovered the following ways for you, too to enjoy a day out with your dog. Remember — DOGS DIE IN HOT CARS!

New Forest horse-drawn wagon rides
These are available in Burley and Brockenhurst from Easter to October. Dogs are allowed on board but must be kept quiet and on leads to avoid startling the horses and disturbing passengers and wild life. The rides take you through parts of the New Forest you would probably never find on your own. Leaflets available from Tourism Departments.

Beaulieu River Cruises from Bucklers Hard
Half-hourly cruises on the *Swiftsure*, a purpose built boat and run from Easter to September. Departure times advertised at the Pier Kiosk, Bucklers Hard. Dogs permitted on board.

Keyhaven to Hurst Castle and Yarmouth IOW by ferryboat
Hourly departures from Keyhaven, Milford on Sea, from May to October. Dogs are allowed on board but not in Hurst Castle which was built by King Henry VIII and once held King Charles I prisoner. This is the nearest point in the mainland to the IOW with fine views of passing ships. There is a large, shingly beach at Hurst Castle where dogs are permitted. I would not recommend returning on foot as the 1½ mile pebble spit makes hard going for little paws.

Cholderton Rare Breeds Farm Park
Open from the end of March to the end of October. To be found off the A338 Salisbury to Marlborough road and signed from the junction of the A338/A303. Established in 1987 and in a picturesque setting, the farm covers 50 acres on the Hants/Wilts border. There are over 50 different breeds of rabbits, plus rare pigs, sheep, goats, poultry, cows, ponies and Shire horses. In high season, the 'Pork Stakes' pig races are held twice daily. Leaflets are available from Tourism Departments

Stewarts Garden Centre, God's Blessing Lane, Broomhill, Holt, Wimborne
A dog-friendly Garden Centre in beautiful Dorset countryside. There are tables outside where you may be with your dog while you have a snack from the café then walk the Nature Trail which runs around the perimeter of the Garden Centre. A safe, off the lead walk if your dog is under control.

Poole Quay Boat Trips
From Easter to October there are many trips to be taken with your dog. I would personally recommend one which cruises around the islands of Poole Harbour with unsurpassed views. (NOTE: dogs are not permitted to land on Brownsea Island).

Lulworth Castle Grounds
The ancestral home of the Weld family, the castle is set in beautiful Lulworth Park. Dogs under control are welcome in the Park but not permitted in the Castle. Wander through ancient woodland and out onto open heath in lovely, unspoilt countryside.

Abbotsbury Sub-Tropical Gardens

Dogs are allowed on leads. Open all year round. Magnificent gardens famed for magnolias, camellias and rhododendrons. There are over 20 acres of wooded valley with walled garden, peacocks, ponds and streams. Many rare plants survive in this unique micro-climate.

A Challenge!

Believe it or not, it is possible to walk from Broadstone to the centre of Bournemouth via heath and pinewoods, mainly off the lead and with only short distances by road. If you are not familiar with the area I suggest taking a street plan with you, but this is the route I chose:

From Broadstone Sports Club take the old railway track bridle path to Delph Woods. Exit at Gravel Hill. Walk in the direction of Poole and enter Canford Heath by the Crematorium, bridle road to Wallisdown. Cross the heath heading east and exit by Knighton Heath Golf Club. Cross over Ringwood Road to Bourne Bottom, follow through to Alder Road. Cross over and take the footpath across Talbot Heath, passing Fern Barrow to East Avenue. Go through Pugs Hole (entrance alongside Talbot Heath School). Exit opposite Walsford Road and enter Meyrick Park Golf Course where a path runs around the perimeter. Exit into Central Drive by the Town Hall. To cheat a little, after Pugs Hole you could cross Branksome Wood Road to Bournemouth Gardens and make your way to the centre of Bournemouth.... Worth a challenge?